anti-stress
MEDITATION THROUGH COLORING

DR STAN RODSKI B.Ec., D.Sc.(BIO)
PEAK PERFORMANCE NEUROSCIENTIST

hardie grant books

About the Authors

Dr Stan Rodski B.Ec., D.Sc(BIO)
Neuroscientist

Stan has worked as a psychologist for over 30 years and most recently he has been involved in neuroscientific research around the issues of stress and how best to deal with it in our personal, family and work life.

He first qualified as a registered psychologist in 1985 and completed his doctorate in Bio Science in 1994.

He has worked in private practice in Australia and internationally, working with individuals, elite sporting teams and many Australian and international Top 500 companies.

Most recently he has been applying brain science research to areas such as improved sleep, fatigue and stress, and energy revitalization and management.

This research has led to a number of programs that he facilitates all over the world. The coloring book series was first available through these programs where its success in creating a calming effect was first recognized and established.

Jack Dowling
Jack is an architecture student at RMIT University in Melbourne, Australia; co-director of online art community, Artselect; and illustrator for the adult coloring series of books. Jack describes finding patterns as a creative and iterative process. He hopes readers will similarly apply their own creative intuition, allowing the mind to relax and enjoy the meditative qualities that come from these exercises.

CONTENTS

INTRODUCTION   4

PART ONE: Brain Science   7

PART TWO: Color   36

PART THREE: New pathways   67

Introduction

Welcome to this mindful improvement approach to stress.

The latest neuroscience research shows that people who pursue creative activities outside their normal home and work duties not only deal with stress better, but their performance also improves, particularly with regard to sleep.

The coloring exercises in this book were developed based on the recognition of the stress relief that being focused on a single activity can bring. Picking up a crayon, pencil or paintbrush and coloring between the lines engages our brain in a focused and mindful task. A task that takes us back to a place in our memory that is carefree and safe.

This mindful activity brings no element of competition or failure, which is very rare for us today. It does, however, create a total absorption in a creative activity that any of us can do.

It only takes 30 minutes a day, and lets you enter a world in which there are no voices, no demands, no thoughts, quite simply enjoying the task and creating – even if you are not creative!

In coloring between the lines we have an activity that is important to the adult brain. The lines, and in particular coloring between the lines, represents 'order and certainty' in our world. When we are stressed, these things are under attack as the world appears chaotic.

So, for 30 minutes a day, practice the mindful technique of coloring. This creative, yet structured approach is what your brain (and you) craves. Enjoy the satisfaction, calmness and better sleep that coloring will bring you.

Dr Stan Rodski – Neuroscientist

PART ONE

Brain Science

HERE WE EXPLORE HOW COLORING PRODUCES NATURALLY
CALMING AND RELAXING ALPHA BRAIN WAVES. THE REASON
FOR THIS IS THAT WHEN YOU COLOR, YOU ENTER A
MEDITATIVE STATE ENCOURAGED BY THREE KEY ELEMENTS
OF BRAIN RECUPERATION. THESE INCLUDE THE DESIRE FOR:
— PATTERN
— REPETITION
— CREATIVITY

CREATING A MEDITATIVE STATE IS PRODUCED BY BEING
SINGLE-FOCUSED ON THE GEOMETRIC AND REPETITIVE
PATTERNS WE HAVE CREATED. CREATIVITY IS NATURALLY
PRODUCED AS YOU CHOOSE COLORS. EVERY INDIVIDUAL
CREATES A UNIQUE DESIGN THROUGH COLOR, WHICH IS
MENTALLY SOOTHING.

THE BRAIN SCIENCE BEHIND THIS BOOK

IF WE THINK OF OUR BRAIN AS THE 'GEARS OF A CAR', THE BRAIN'S ROLE IS TO ENSURE WE ARE IN THE RIGHT 'GEAR' FOR OUR NEEDS.

FOR EXAMPLE, WHEN WE GO UP A STEEP HILL IN A CAR, THE GEARS OF OUR CAR SENSE THE PRESSURE ON THE SYSTEM AND GO DOWN TO HELP US UP THE HILL. OUR BRAIN WORKS IN MUCH THE SAME WAY, SO WHENEVER IT PERCEIVES PRESSURE, THE BRAIN ADJUSTS TO THE CIRCUMSTANCES (UPHILL AND DOWNHILL) WE FIND OURSELVES IN. ONCE THE CAR GETS TO THE TOP OF THE HILL IT REVERTS BACK TO ITS 'OPTIMAL' GEAR TO MOVE ALONG.

WHAT WOULD HAPPEN IF OUR GEAR DIDN'T CHANGE BACK BUT CONTINUED TO 'REV' AS IF IT WERE STILL GOING UP THE HILL? IT WOULD VERY QUICKLY OVERHEAT AND BREAK DOWN.

IF OUR BRAIN IS UNABLE TO ADJUST TO THE CHANGES OF PRESSURE, IT ALSO EXPERIENCES 'OVERHEATING' AND 'BREAKDOWN' AND AT ITS WORST CREATES ANXIETY, DEPRESSION AND INSOMNIA. FOR MOST OF US, THE EFFECT OF THIS SUSTAINED PRESSURE IS THE FEELING OF STRESS, LOWER WELLBEING AND SOMETIMES POOR SLEEP - THE BRAIN IS JUST NOT CHANGING GEARS AT THE RIGHT TIME OR FOR THE RIGHT AMOUNT OF TIME.

LET'S LOOK AT THESE 'GEARS' IN THE BRAIN A LITTLE MORE CLOSELY.

THE BRAIN'S 'GEARS' ARE CALLED BRAIN WAVES AND THESE WAVES ARE PRODUCED TO HELP US FUNCTION AT THE RIGHT LEVEL FOR OUR NEEDS. BELOW YOU CAN SEE THE BRAINWAVES REQUIRED BY US TO FUNCTION NORMALLY.

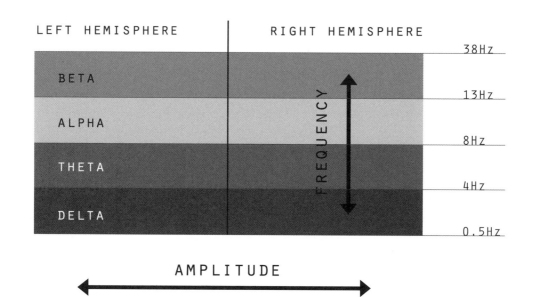

BRAIN WAVES & CONSCIOUSNESS

LEFT HEMISPHERE | RIGHT HEMISPHERE

BETA — 38Hz / 13Hz
ALPHA — 8Hz
THETA — 4Hz
DELTA — 0.5Hz

FREQUENCY

AMPLITUDE

THESE BRAIN WAVES OPERATE FOR THE SITUATION. FOR EXAMPLE, WHEN
WE ARE RELAXED THE PREDOMINANT WAVE IS ALPHA BUT CHANGES TO BETA
AS WE INCREASE BOTH OUR PHYSICAL AND MENTAL ACTIVITY (SEE BELOW).

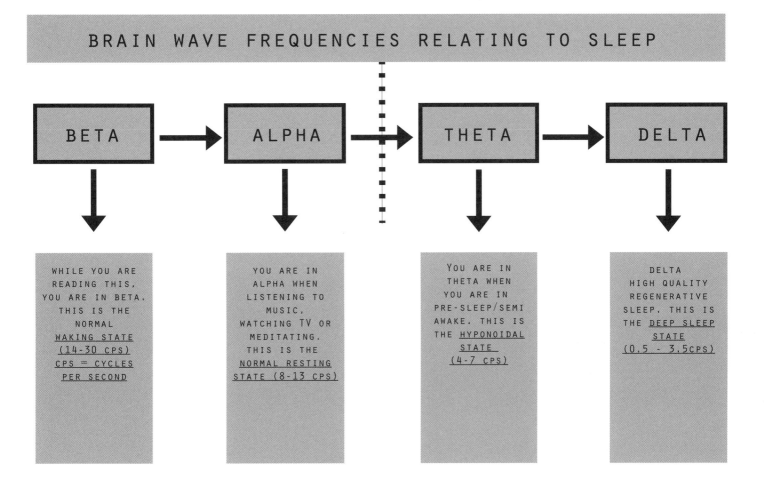

WHEN THE BRAIN NEEDS TO SLEEP WE MOVE TO THETA, AND THEN TO
DELTA BRAINWAVES. THE ABOVE TABLE SHOWS OUR BRAINWAVES AS WE
MOVE FROM WAKEFULNESS TO SLEEP. AT DELTA, THE BRAIN
REPLENISHES ITS ENERGY.

THE REASONS WHY THE BRAIN SOMETIMES DOESN'T SWITCH GEARS BY
ITSELF WHEN IT SHOULD ARE NOT YET FULLY UNDERSTOOD. HOWEVER,
WE HAVE MADE SIGNIFICANT ADVANCES IN HELPING THE BRAIN TO
'SWITCH GEARS'.

THIS BOOK IS DESIGNED TO HELP YOU DO JUST THAT. BRAIN STUDIES
SHOW US THAT WHEN UNDER PRESSURE WE CAN MANUALLY 'CHANGE
GEARS'. BY FOCUSING ON THE TASK OF COLORING BETWEEN THE LINES
WE CAN CHANGE OUR BRAINWAVES FROM BEING IN A CONTINUAL STATE
OF BETA (PRESSURED AND STRESSED) TO A MORE RELAXED STATE OF ALPHA.
THE EFFECTS TO BOTH YOUR HEALTH (PHYSICAL AND MENTAL) AND
PERFORMANCE WHEN YOU'RE PRESSURED WILL BE IMMEDIATELY FELT.

TIME TO
RELAX...

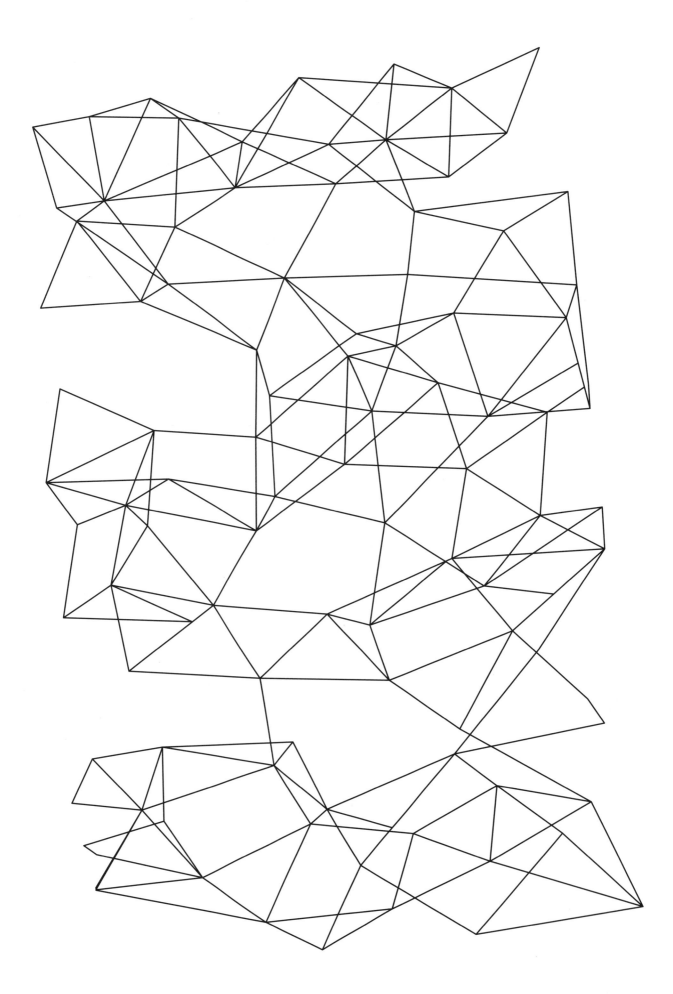

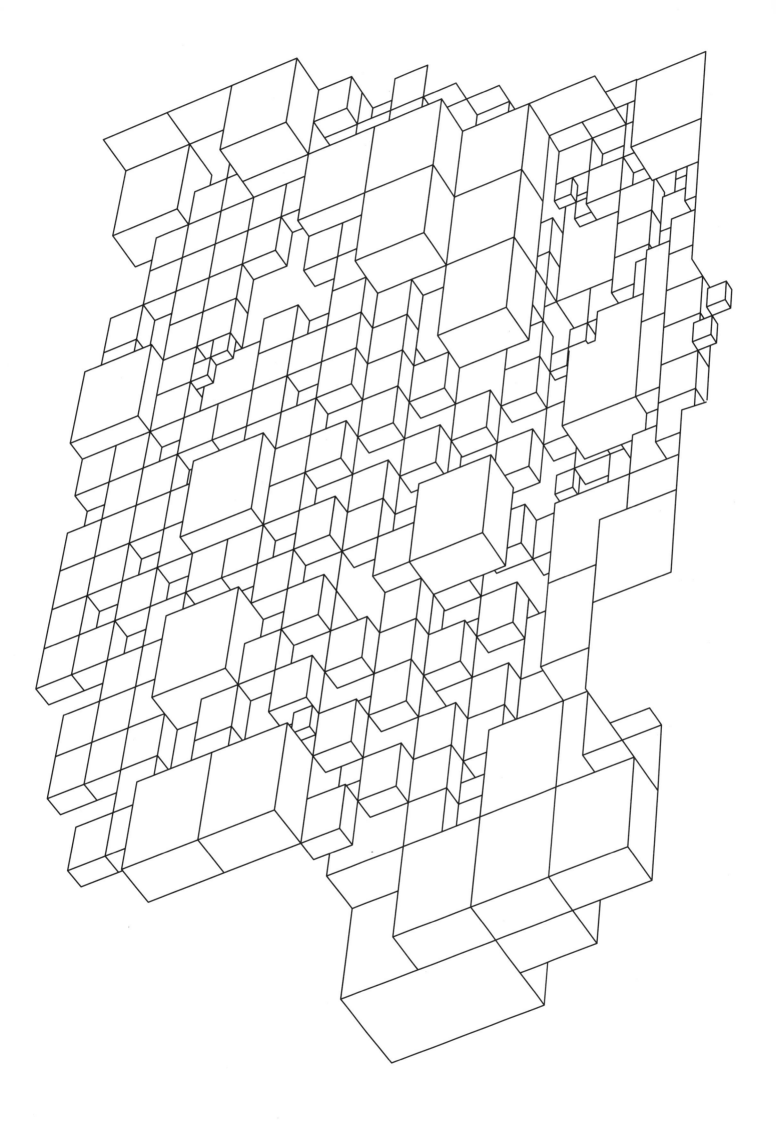

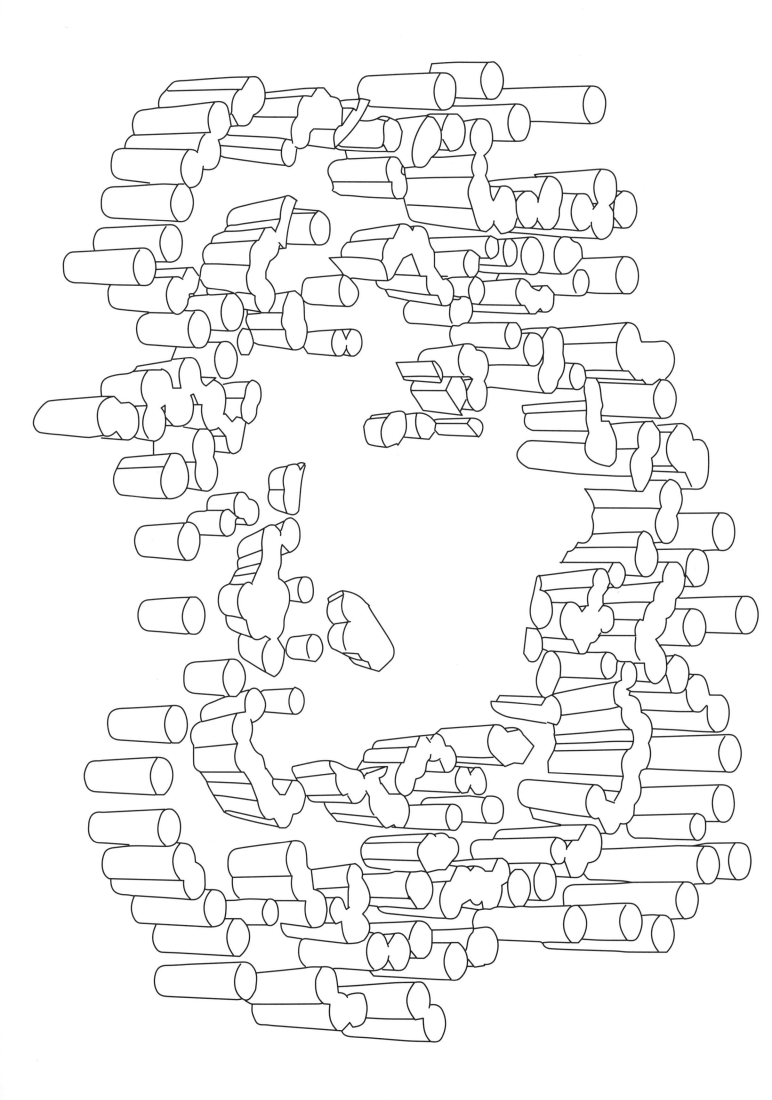

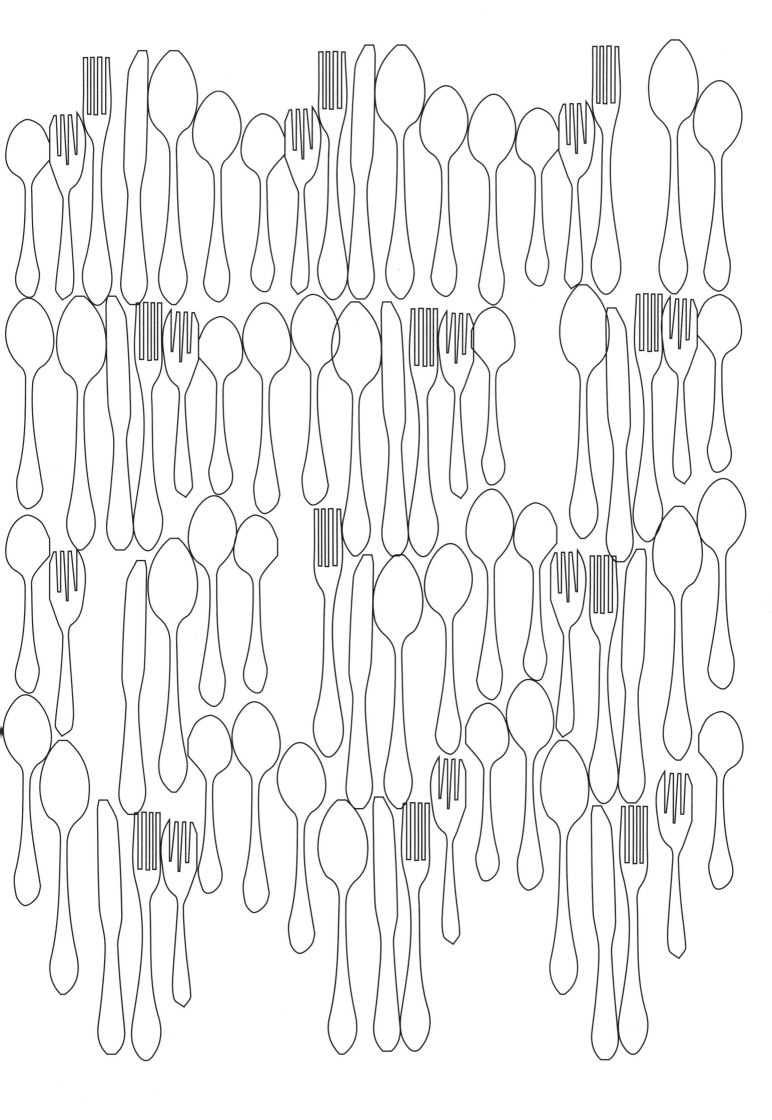

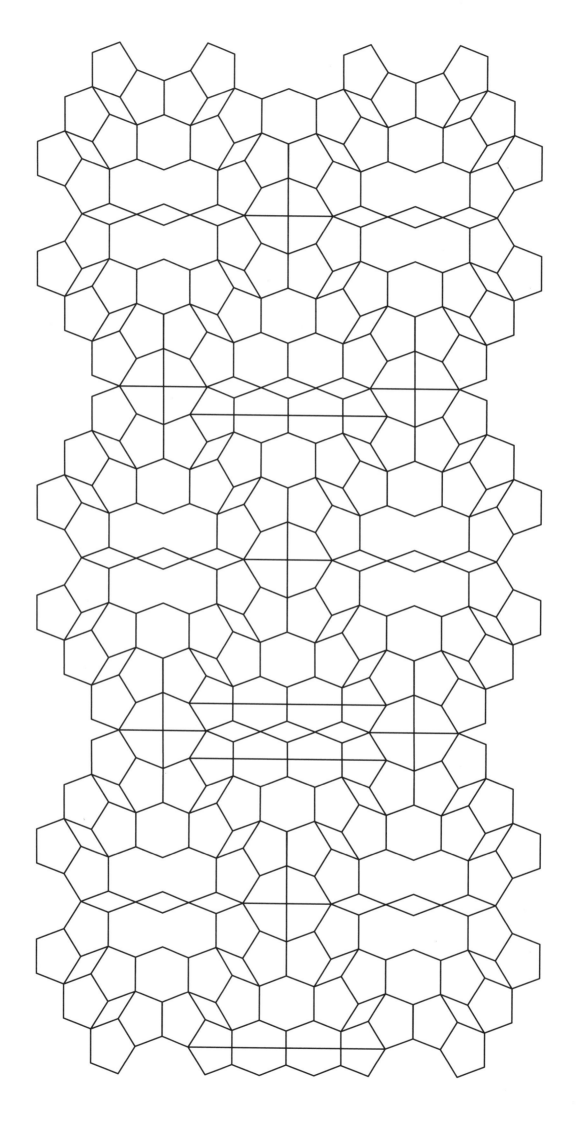

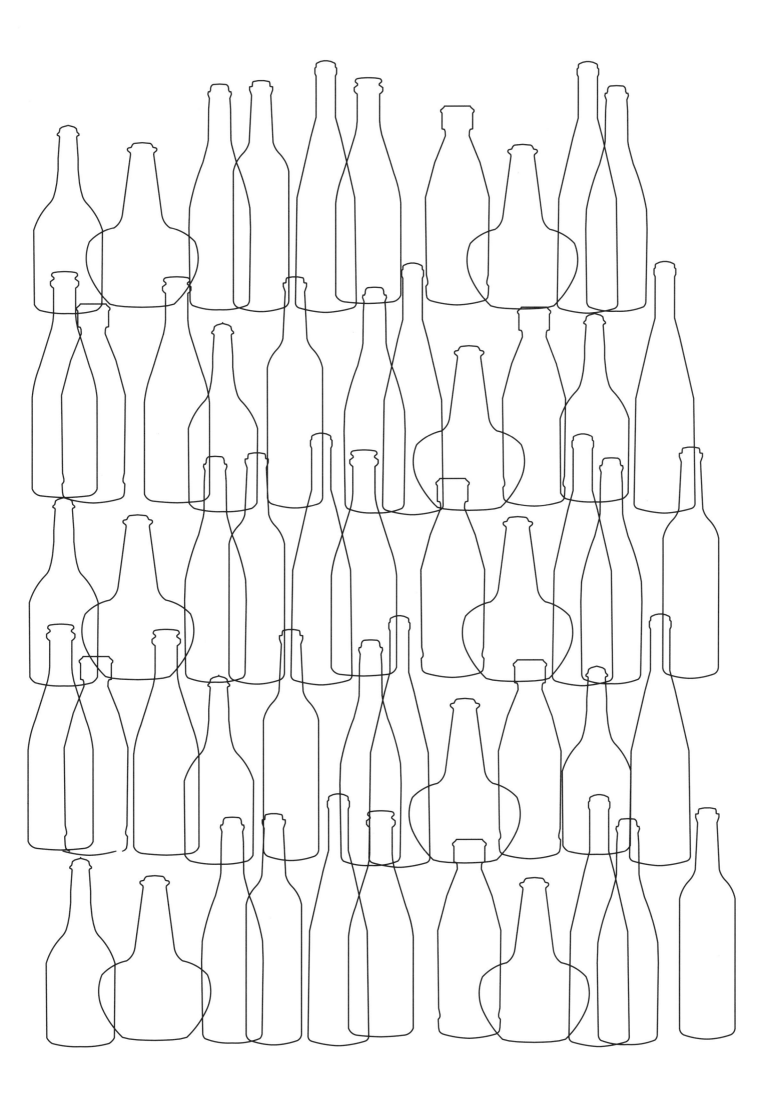

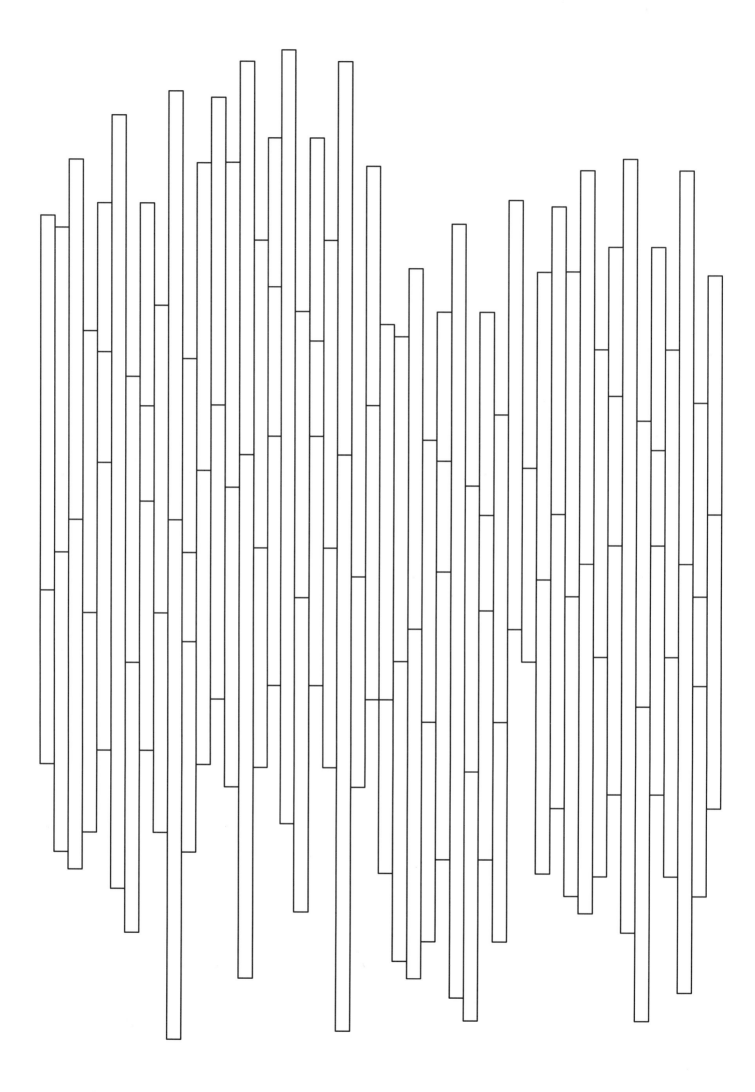

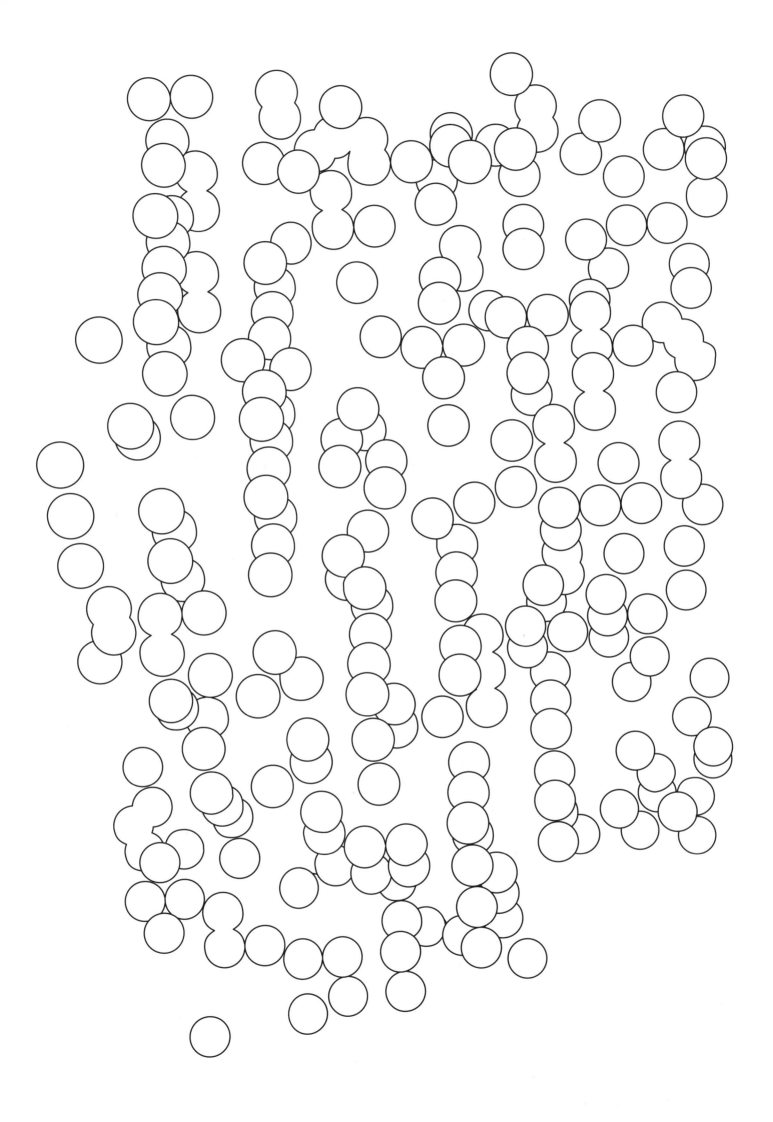

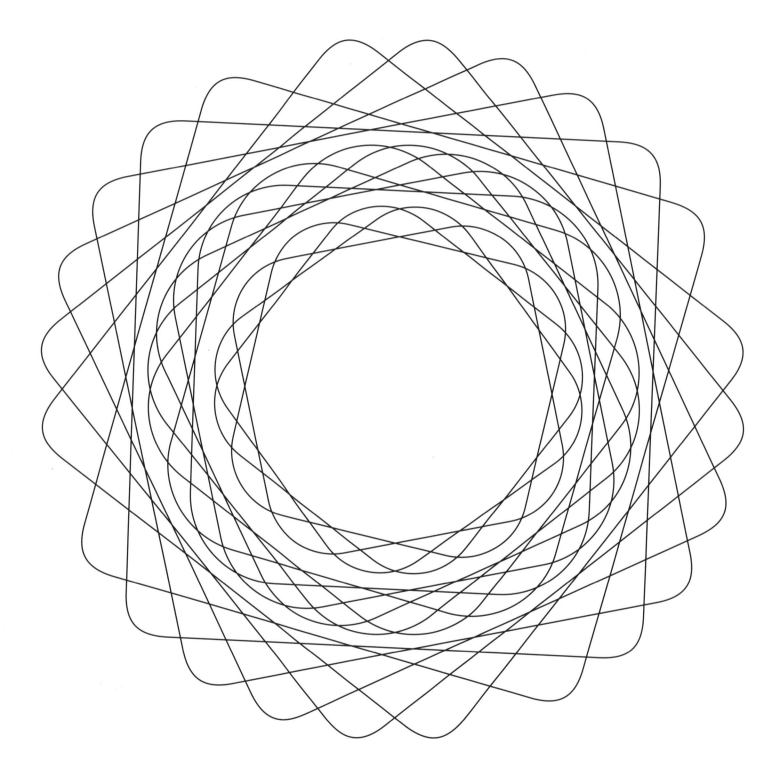

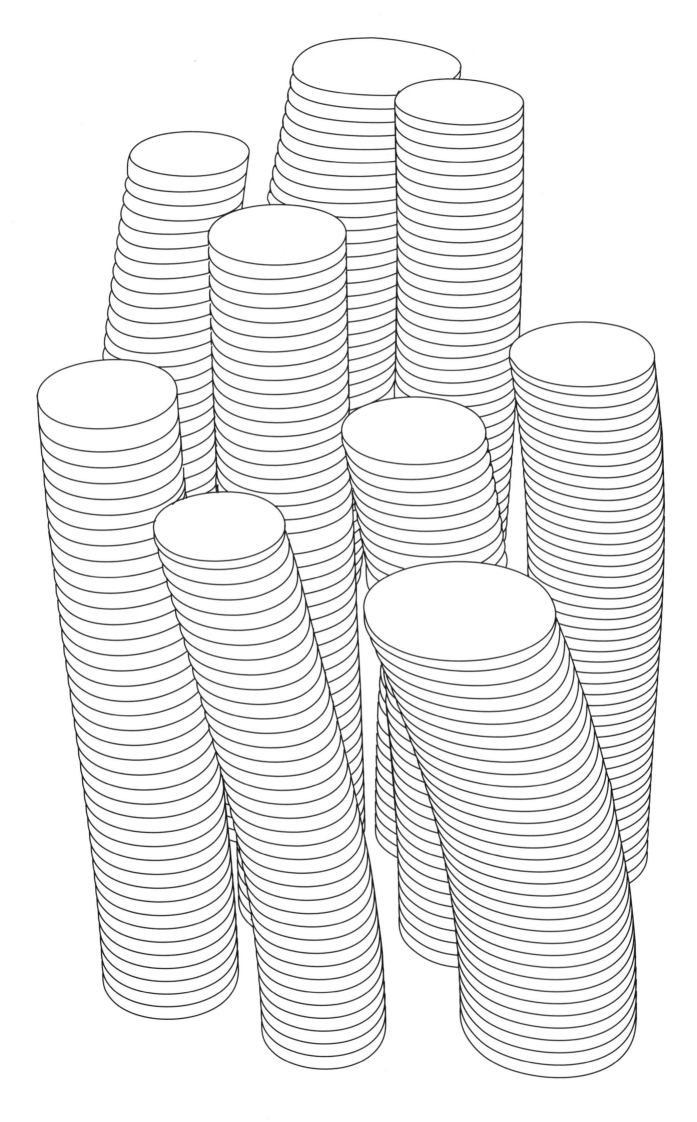

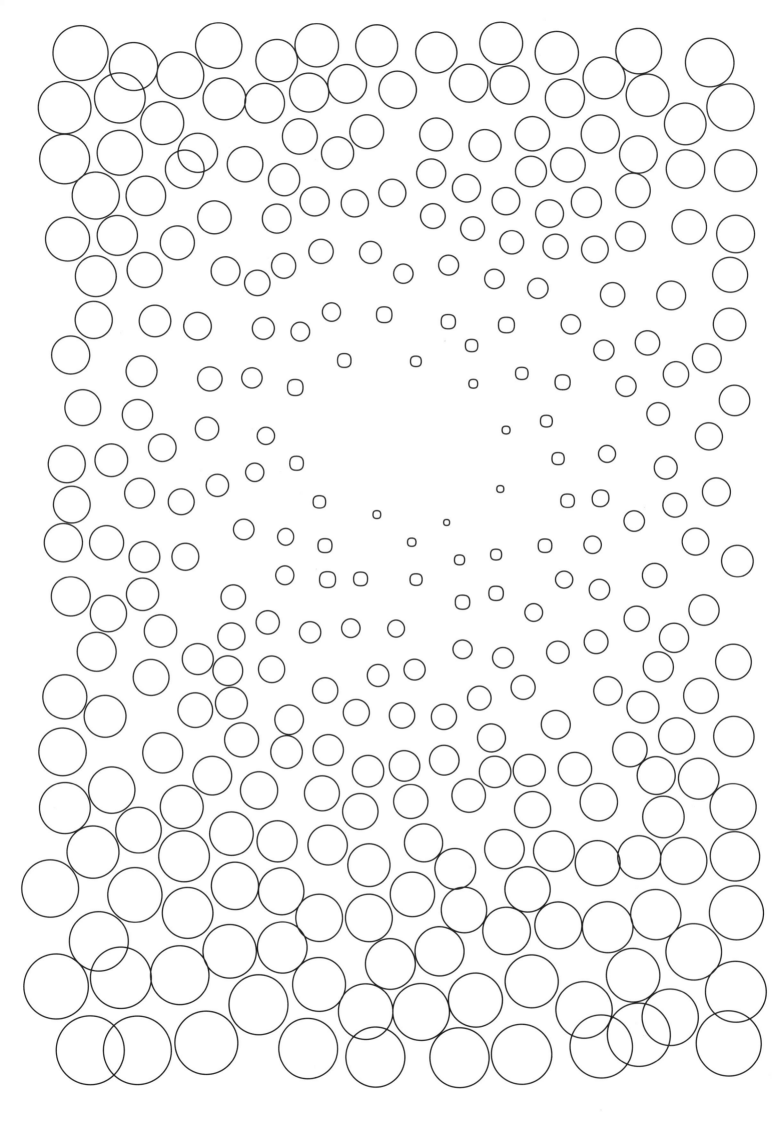

PART TWO

Color

HERE, WE EXPLORE THE ROLE OF COLOR IN THE BRAIN AND THE RESULTANT BEHAVIORS INCLUDING MOOD AND PERSONALITY, WHICH CAN REFLECT OR INDICATE OUR FUTURE THINKING AND BEHAVIORS.

BY COMPLETING THE SHORT COLOR TEST, YOU CAN SEE WHAT YOUR CURRENT COLOR CHOICES SAY ABOUT YOU.

THINKING ABOUT YOUR COLOR CHOICES AND THE MOOD YOU WISH TO ACHIEVE WILL HELP YOUR BRAIN WAVES TOWARDS RELAXATION AND CALM.

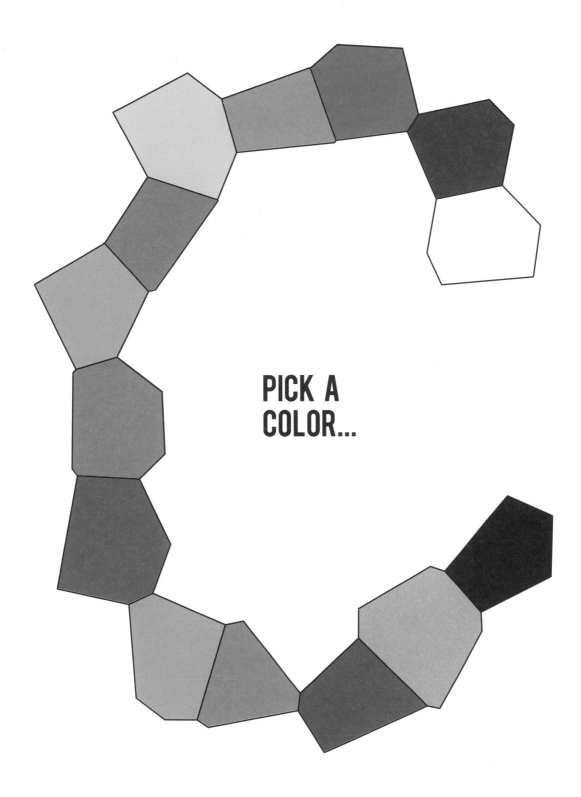

PICK A
COLOR...

COLOR AFFECTS THE WAY YOU FEEL!

IN FACT, IT NOT ONLY AFFECTS THE WAY WE FEEL, BUT THE WAY WE BEHAVE. THE BRAIN SCIENCE BEHIND THIS UNDERSTANDS THAT WHEN LIGHT REFLECTS FROM COLORED OBJECTS AND STRIKES THE RETINAS IN OUR EYES, THE WAVELENGTHS ARE CONVERTED INTO ELECTRICAL IMPULSES. THESE MOVE INTO THE PART OF THE BRAIN THAT RULES OUR HORMONAL ENDOCRINE SYSTEM. IT IS THIS SYSTEM WHICH REGULATES OUR MOODS. UNCONSCIOUSLY, THEN, OUR EYES AND BODIES CONSTANTLY ADAPT TO THESE STIMULI, ALTERING OUR IMPULSES AND PERCEPTIONS THROUGH COLOR-EVOKED HORMONE ACTIVITY.

LET'S LOOK AT WHAT EMOTIONS CAN BE EVOKED BY COLOR. IN PARTICULAR, CONSIDER THE COLOR YOU PICKED AND WHAT THIS SAYS ABOUT YOU...

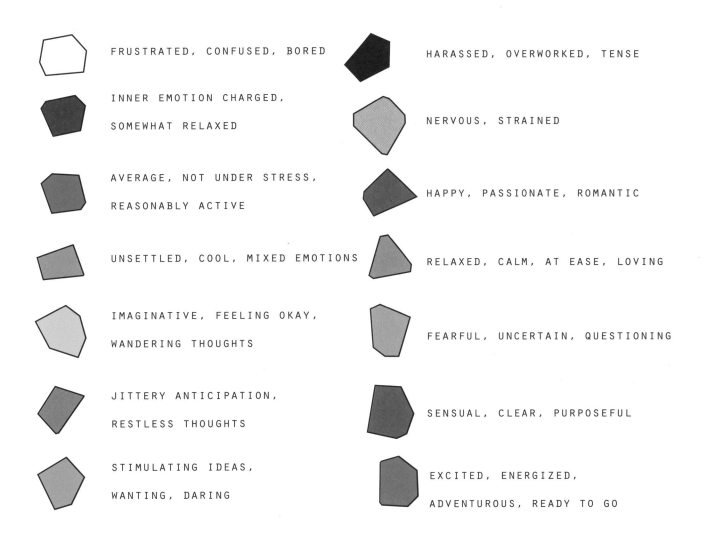

FRUSTRATED, CONFUSED, BORED

HARASSED, OVERWORKED, TENSE

INNER EMOTION CHARGED,
SOMEWHAT RELAXED

NERVOUS, STRAINED

AVERAGE, NOT UNDER STRESS,
REASONABLY ACTIVE

HAPPY, PASSIONATE, ROMANTIC

UNSETTLED, COOL, MIXED EMOTIONS

RELAXED, CALM, AT EASE, LOVING

IMAGINATIVE, FEELING OKAY,
WANDERING THOUGHTS

FEARFUL, UNCERTAIN, QUESTIONING

JITTERY ANTICIPATION,
RESTLESS THOUGHTS

SENSUAL, CLEAR, PURPOSEFUL

STIMULATING IDEAS,
WANTING, DARING

EXCITED, ENERGIZED,
ADVENTUROUS, READY TO GO

WHEN COLORING, BE MINDFUL OF THE EMOTIONS THAT ARE BEING EVOKED
WHILE YOU RELAX... HAPPY COLORING!

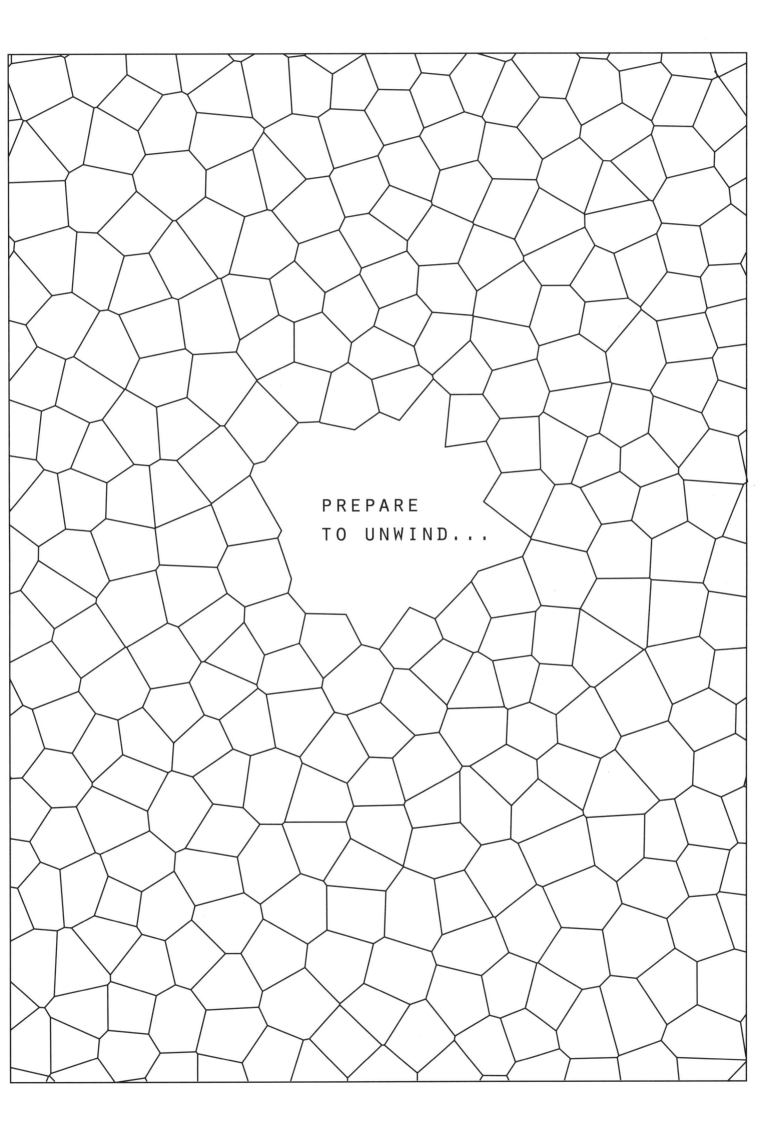

PREPARE
TO UNWIND...

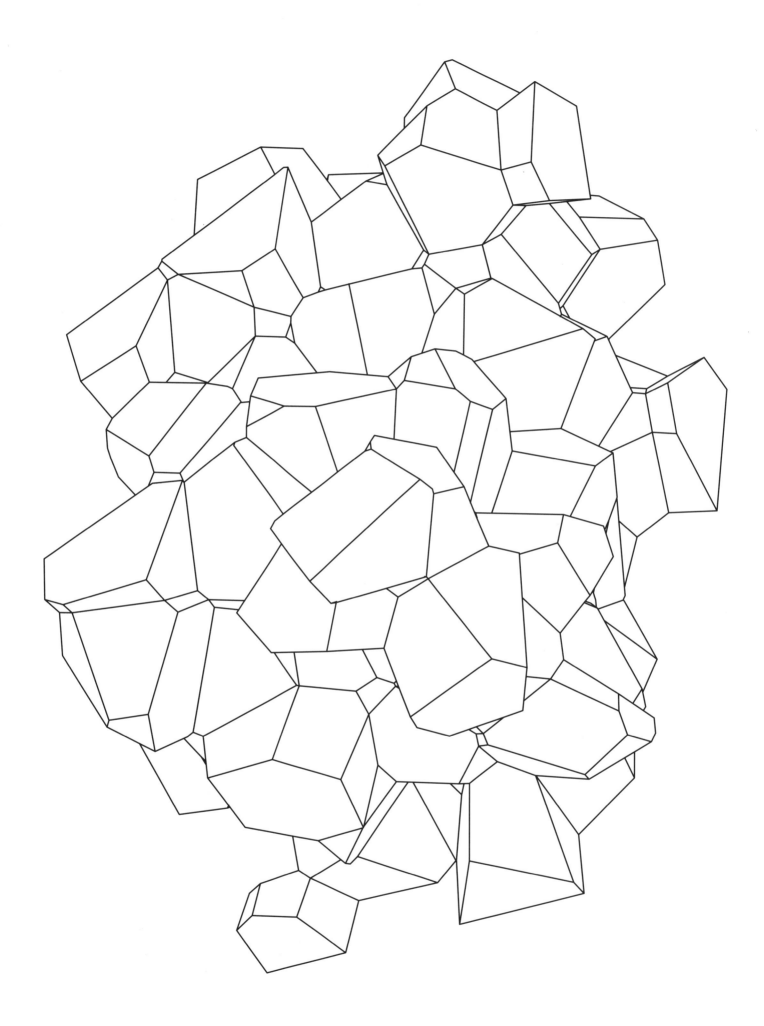

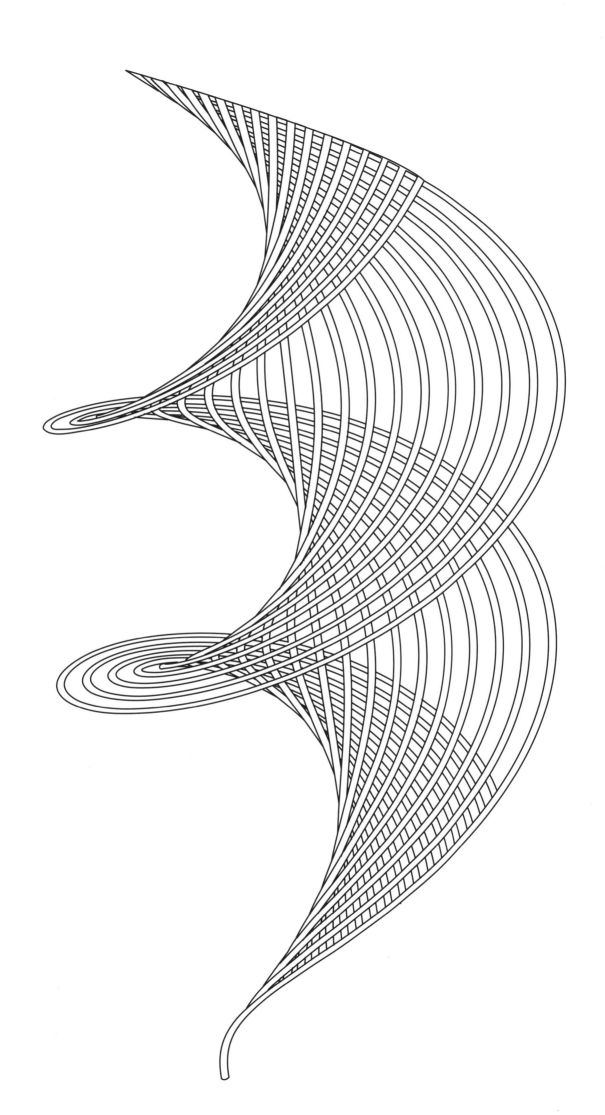

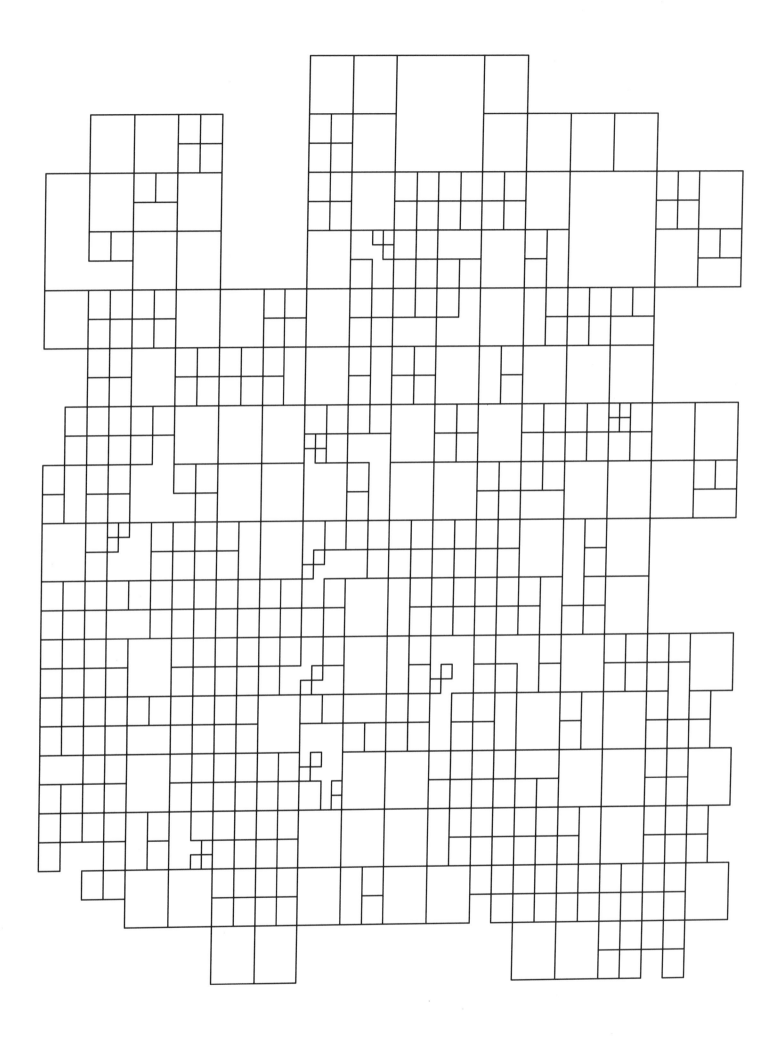

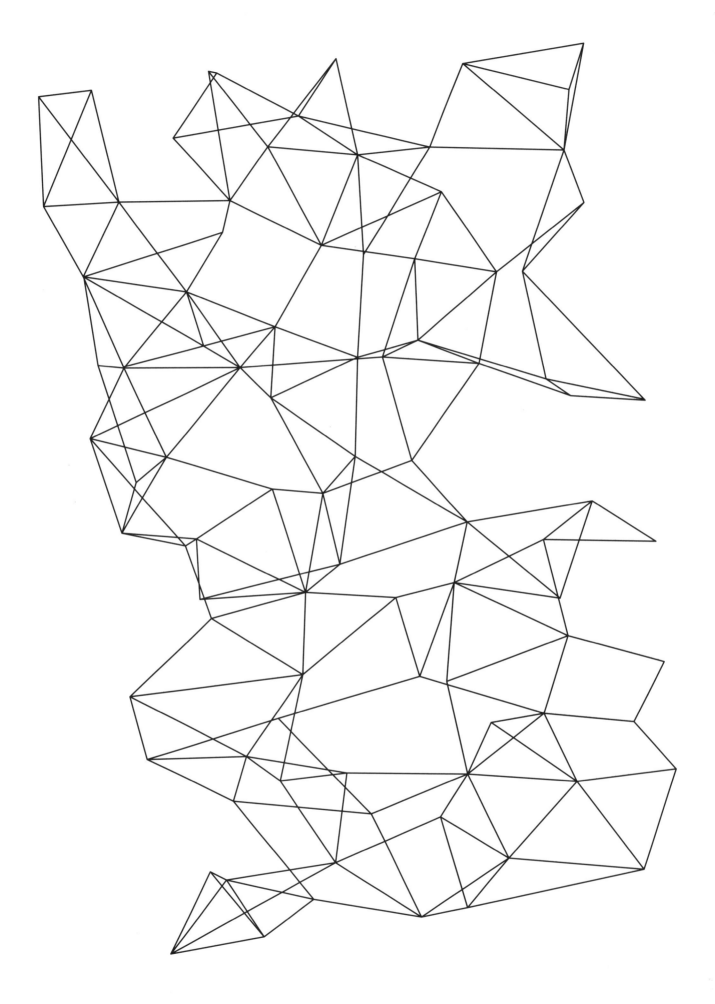

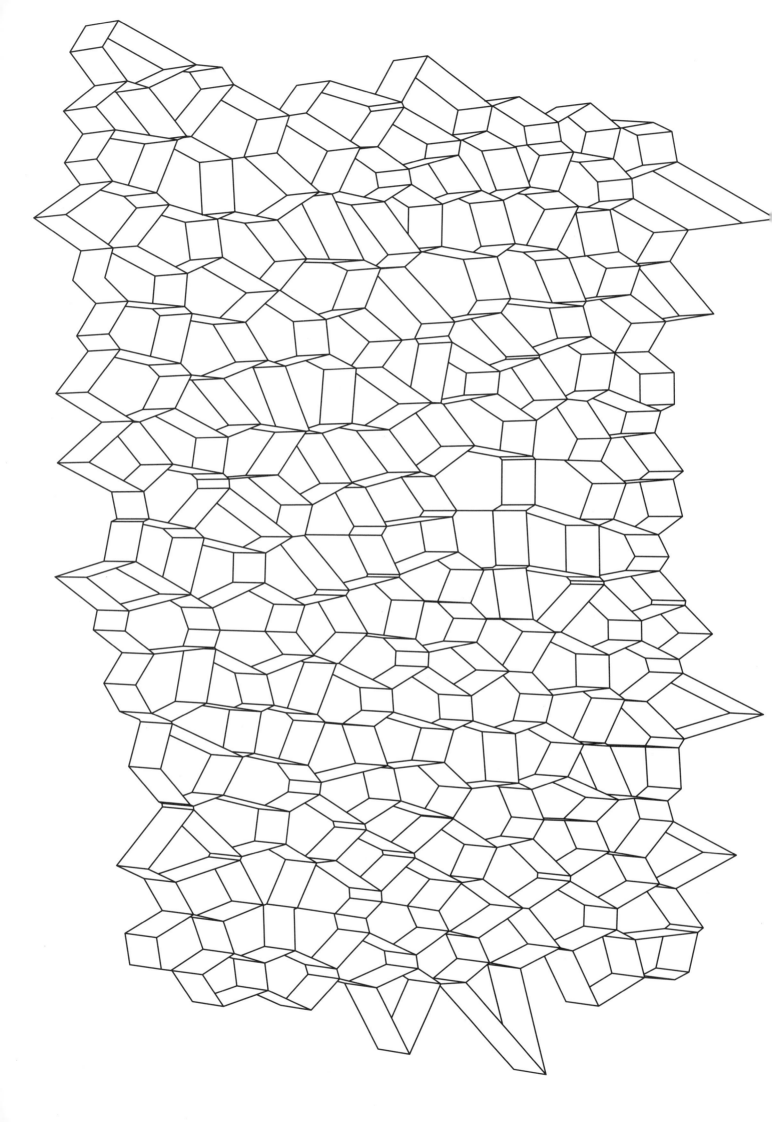

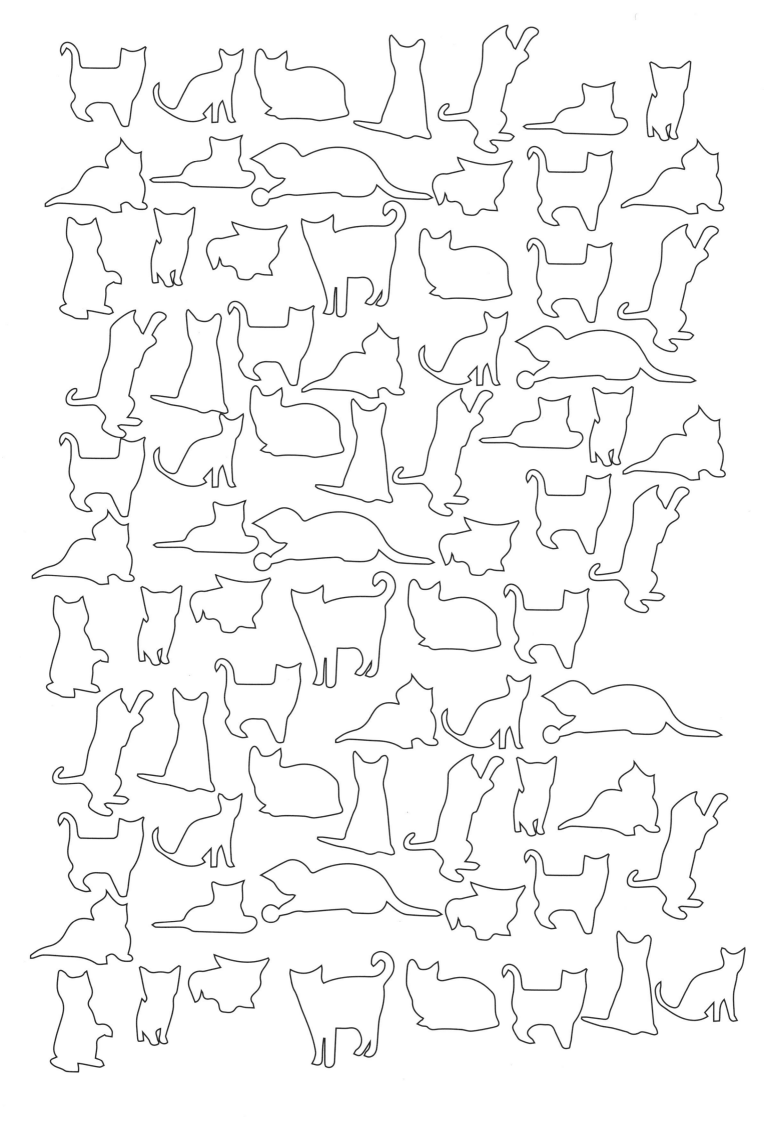

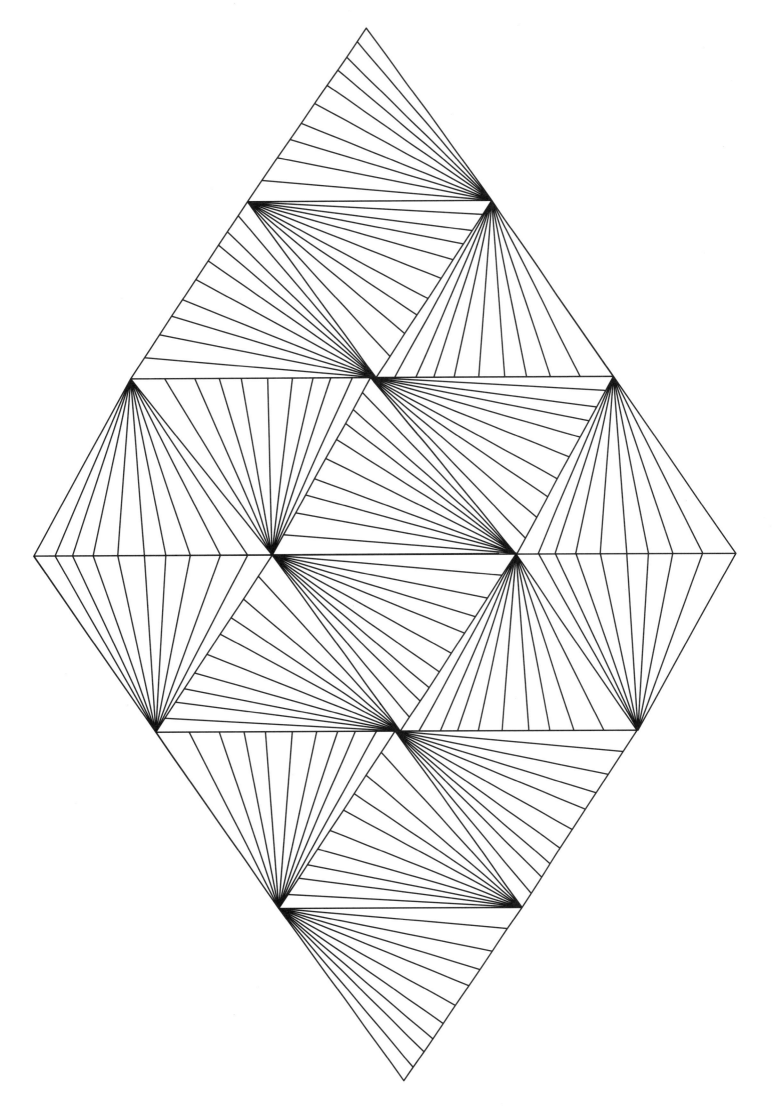

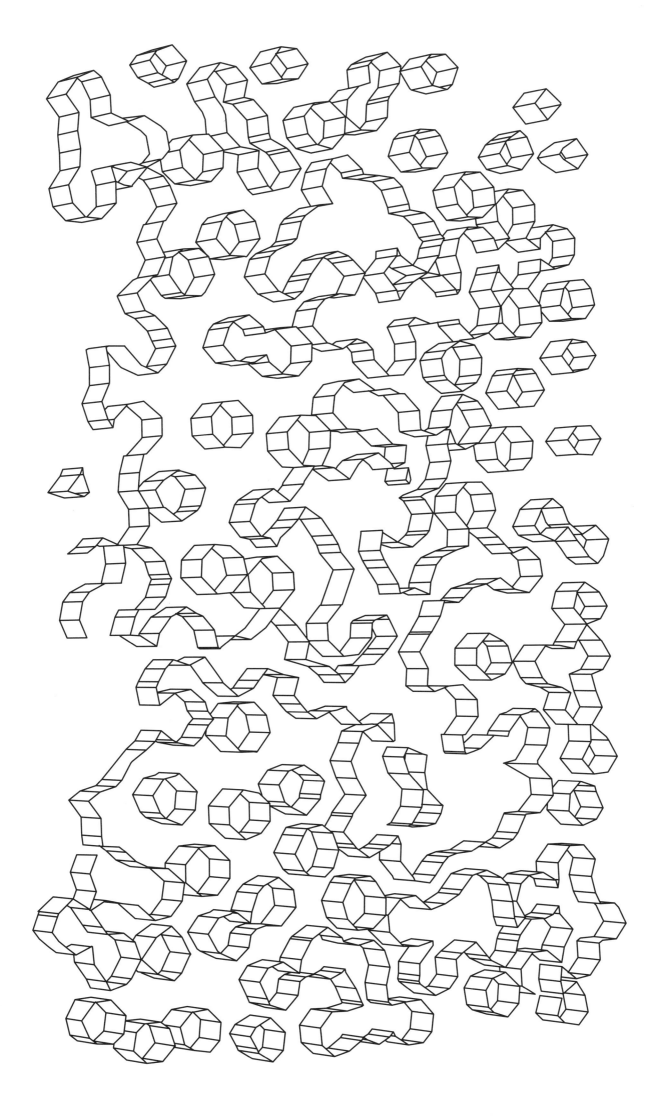

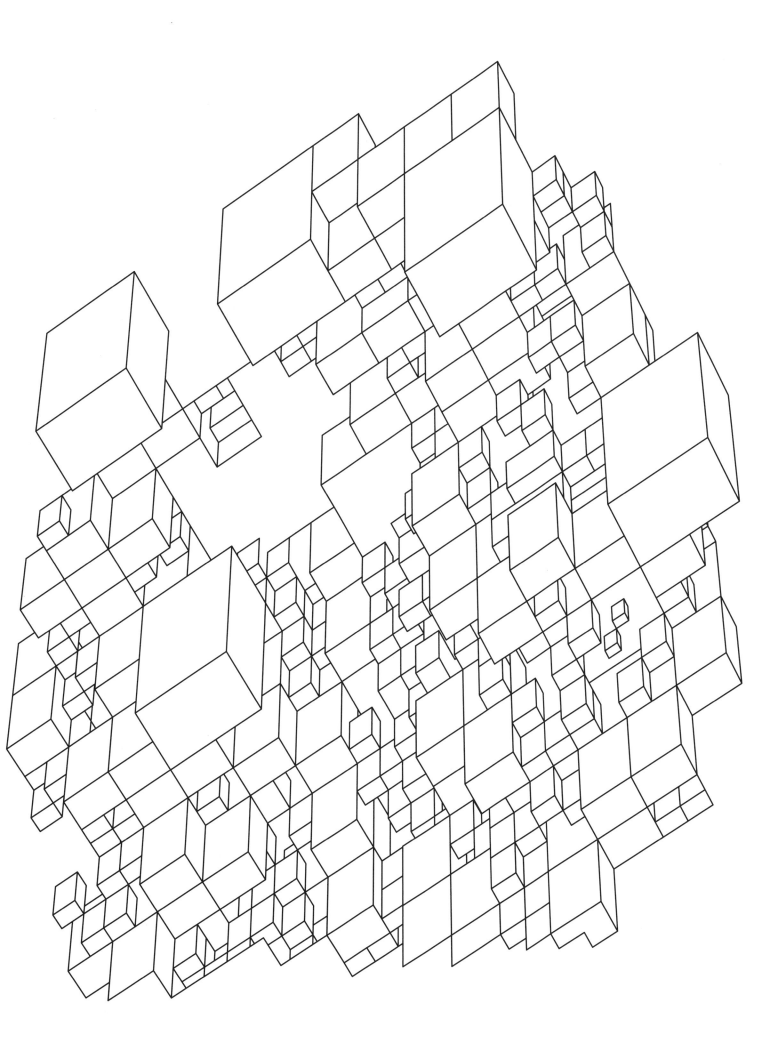

PART THREE

New pathways

IN THIS THIRD PART WE EXPLORE HOW TO STIMULATE OUR BRAIN AFTER ACHIEVING AN ALPHA STATE AND BEING MINDFUL OF THE MOOD AND EMOTION WE FIND OURSELVES IN. USING COLORING AS A MINDFUL IMPROVEMENT APPROACH TO STRESS, WE ENCOURAGE YOU TO STIMULATE YOUR BRAIN BY PRACTICING THE EXERCISES ON THE FOLLOWING PAGES. THEY WILL ENABLE YOU TO TAKE ADVANTAGE OF YOUR NEW-FOUND ABILITY TO ACHIEVE A RELAXED STATE COMBINED WITH EVEN BETTER BRAIN PERFORMANCE.

HAPPY COLORING AND ENJOY PRACTICING YOUR BRAIN EXERCISES TO KEEP YOUR BRAIN HEALTHY AND PERFORMING AT ITS OPTIMUM.

STIMULATING OUR BRAIN FOR HEALTHY PERFORMANCE

OUR BRAIN IS ORGANIZED BY WHAT WE CALL IN NEUROSCIENCE 'CROSS LATERALIZATION'. THIS BASICALLY MEANS THAT THE LEFT SIDE OF OUR BRAIN CONTROLS MANY FUNCTIONS ON THE RIGHT SIDE OF OUR BODY AND VICE VERSA FOR THE RIGHT SIDE.

WHEN WE ENTER A MEDITATIVE STATE PRODUCED BY COLORING, WE ALSO NEED TO RECOGNIZE THE NEED TO RESUME OUR MENTAL FUNCTIONING AND THINKING, SO WE CAN GET ON WITH OUR LIFE.

BECAUSE OF THE STRESSES IN OUR LIVES, WE NEED TO NOT ONLY LEARN TO RELAX BUT ALSO TO THINK ABOUT OUR ISSUES IN NEW AND CREATIVE WAYS TO REDUCE OUR STRESS IN THE LONG TERM.

THE FIRST BRAIN STIMULATION EXERCISE WE NEED TO DO IS TO SIMPLY CHANGE HANDS WHEN COLORING. IF YOU NORMALLY COLOR WITH YOUR RIGHT HAND, CHANGE TO THE LEFT, AND VICE VERSA IF YOU ARE LEFT HANDED.

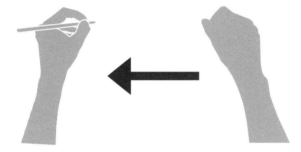

THIS WILL STIMULATE NEURONS IN YOUR OTHER HEMISPHERE AND CREATE NEW PATHWAYS FOR YOU TO LOOK AT YOUR ISSUES IN DIFFERENT WAYS. TODAY THIS IS OFTEN REFERRED TO AS NEUROPLASTICITY, WHICH IS AN EVOLVING AND EXCITING BRANCH OF NEUROSCIENCE. FOR THE SECOND EXERCISE, TRY COLORING USING BOTH HANDS AT THE SAME TIME.

START BY COLORING AREAS WHICH ARE QUITE CLOSE TO EACH OTHER, AND AS YOU IMPROVE, MOVE TO DIFFERENT COLORS MUCH FURTHER APART.

FINALLY, REMEMBER TO USE THIS TECHNIQUE AT THE END OF YOUR COLORING SESSION. ONCE YOU HAVE ACHIEVED A RELAXED STATE BY COLORING CREATIVELY FOR 25 MINUTES, THE FINAL 5 MINUTES CAN BE USED TO AWAKEN BOTH HEMISPHERES OF YOUR BRAIN AND PREPARE YOU TO FIND THE ENERGY AND SOLUTIONS FOR THOSE THINGS THAT ARE CAUSING STRESS IN YOUR LIFE.

HAVE FUN WITH IT AND DON'T GIVE UP. YOU WILL GET BETTER!

HAPPY RELAXED AND CREATIVE COLORING.

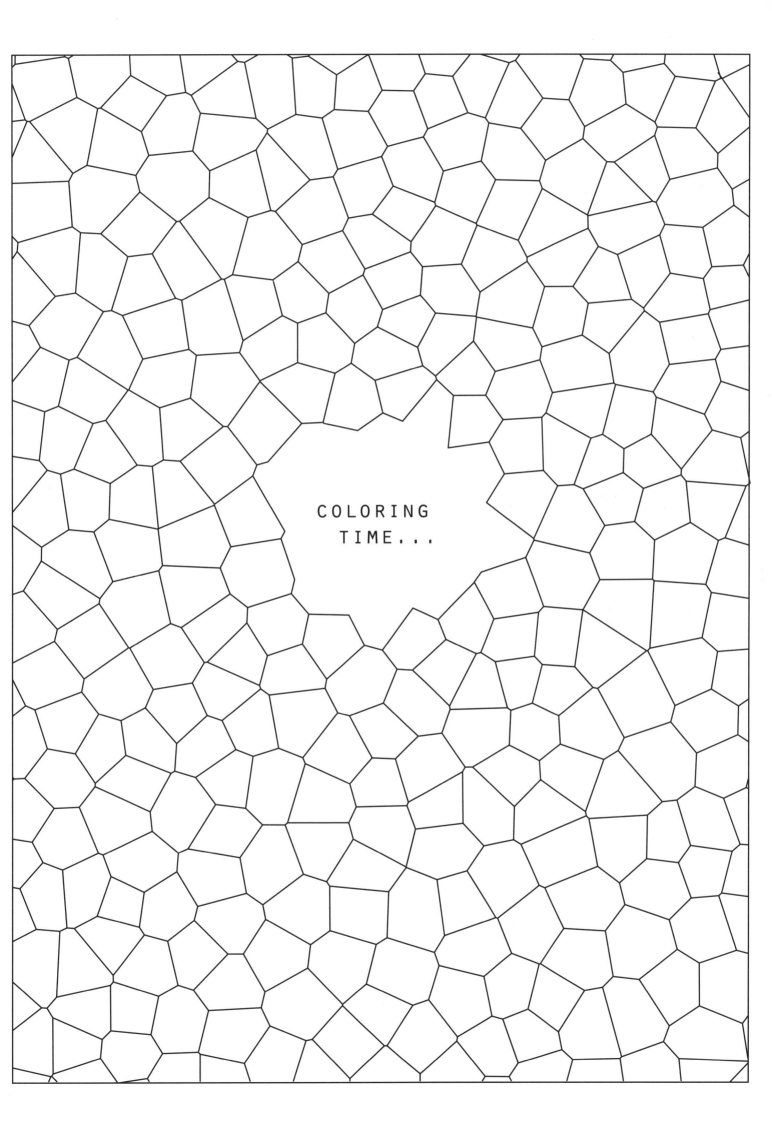

COLORING
TIME...

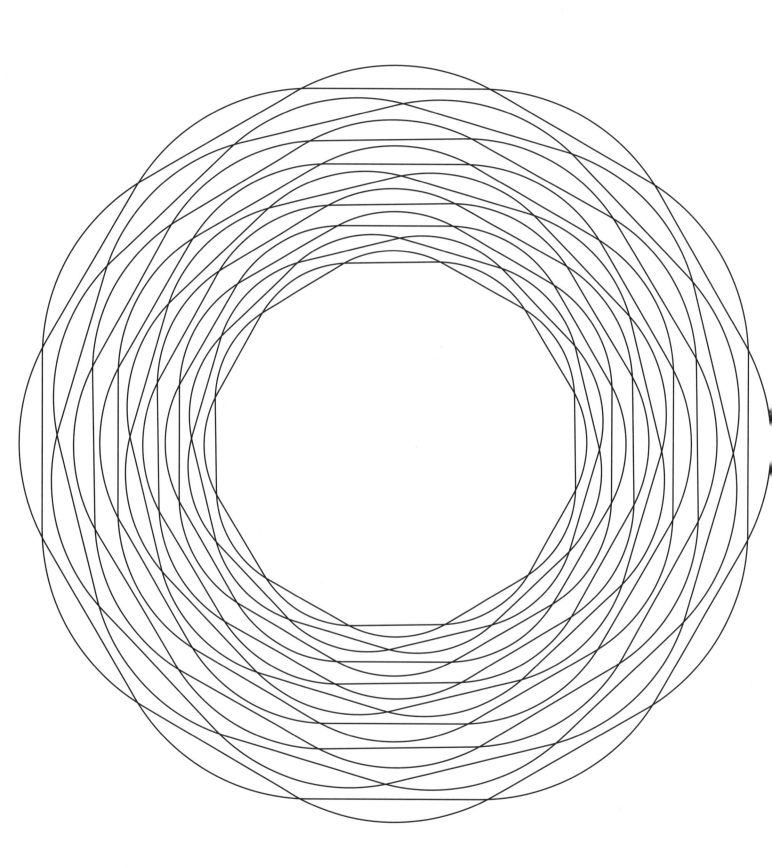

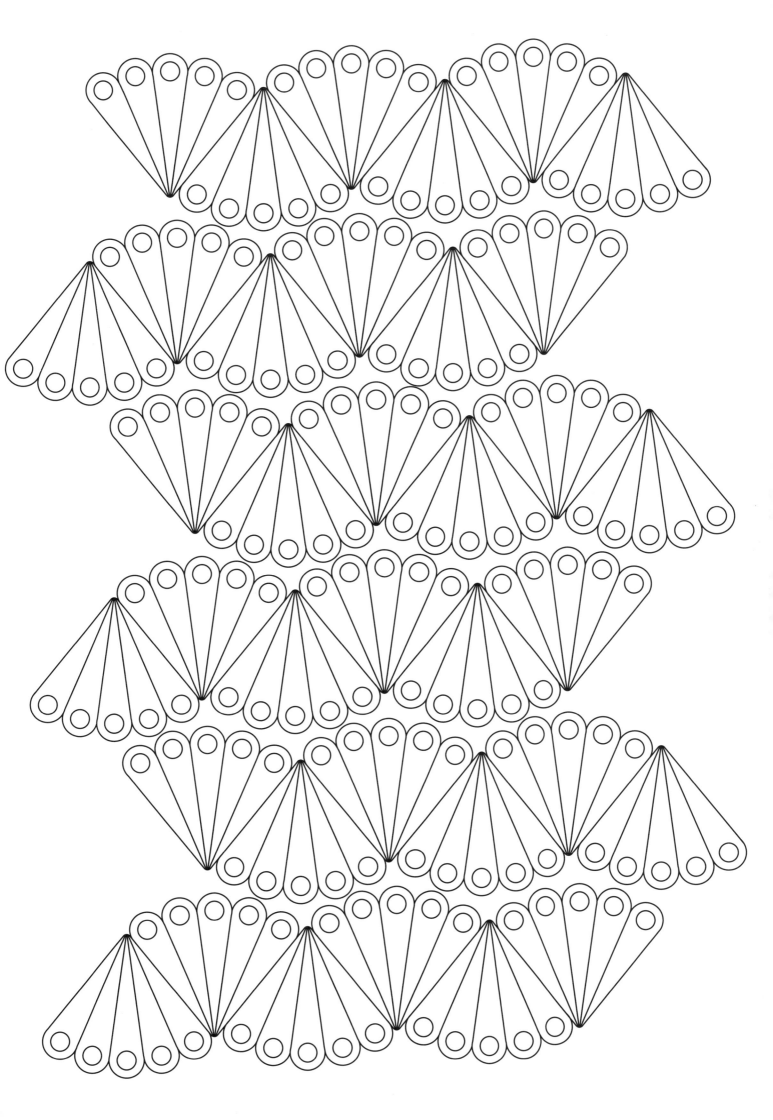

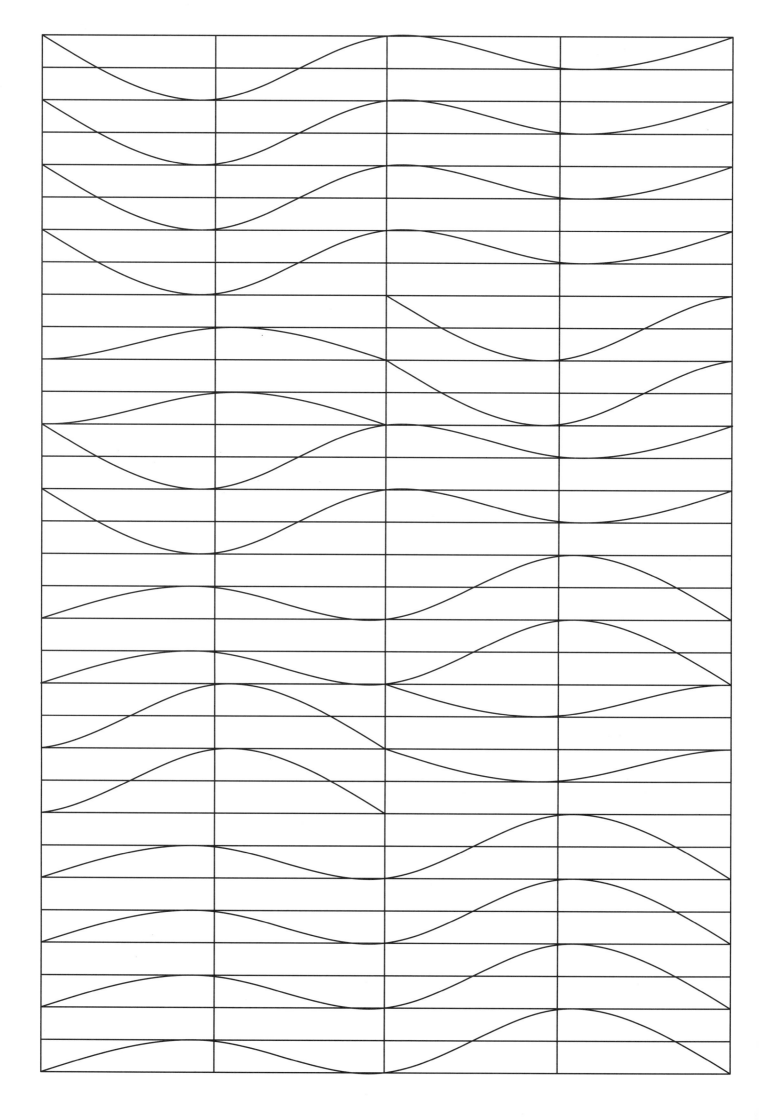

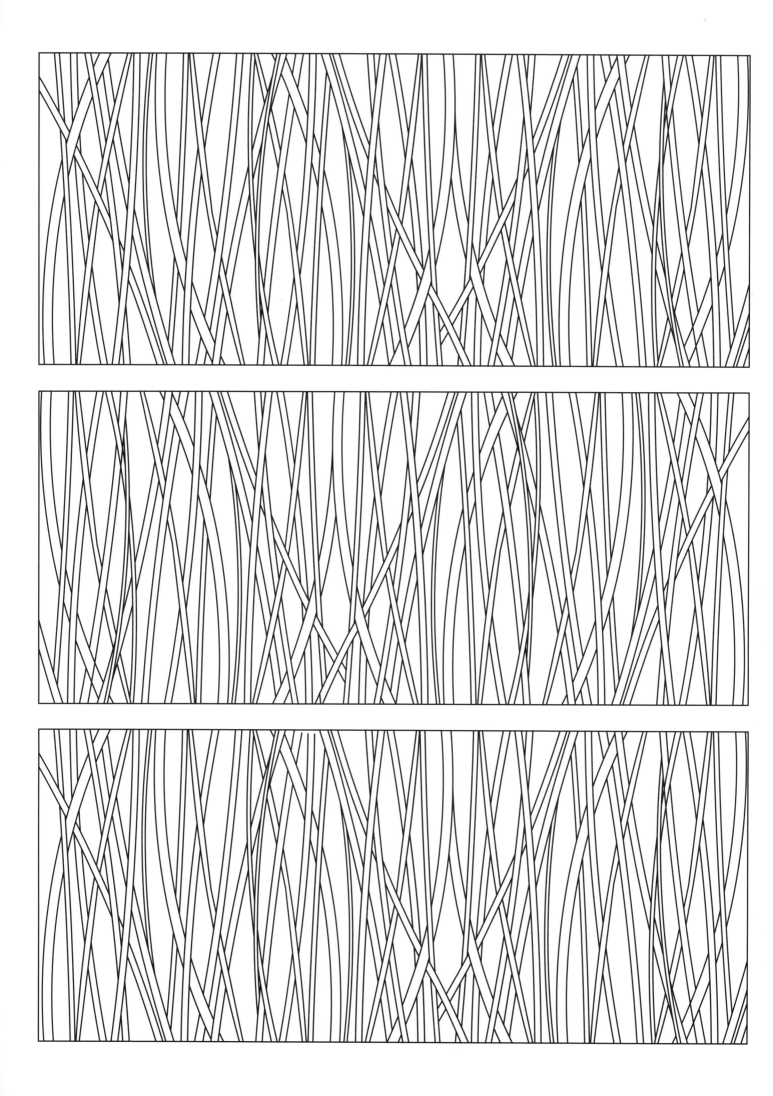

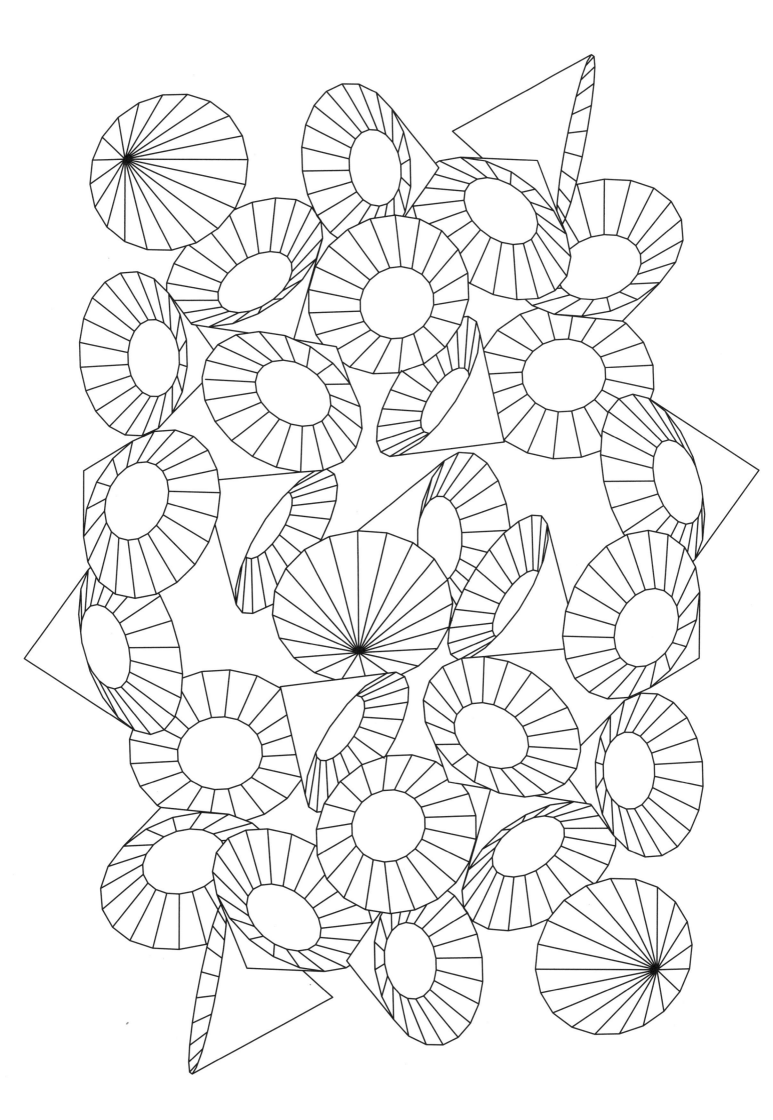

Published in 2015 by Hardie Grant Books
This edition published in 2016

Hardie Grant Books (Australia)
Ground Floor, Building 1
658 Church Street
Richmond, Victoria 3121
www.hardiegrant.com.au

Hardie Grant Books (UK)
5th & 6th Floors
52–54 Southwark Street
London SE1 1UN
www.hardiegrant.co.uk

A Cataloguing-in-Publication entry is available from the catalogue of
the National Library of Australia at www.nla.gov.au
Anti-stress: Meditation through coloring
ISBN 9781743791875
Website: www.colourtation.com
Facebook: www.facebook.com/colourtation
Instagram: @colourtation

Cover, illustrations and text design by Jack Dowling
Printed in China by 1010 Printing International Limited